Python for Little Geniuses: Discover Programming

CARLOS ROLDÁN BLAY

MARTA ROLDÁN CANTI

DEDICATION

This book is lovingly dedicated to my daughter, Marta Roldán Canti.

Marta, at just 10 years old, your enthusiasm and your eagerness to learn and create never cease to amaze me. This book is an adventure we designed together, and it fills me with pride that you are my apprentice and co-author. With your curious spirit and boundless energy, I know this is just the beginning of many other exciting adventures we will share together in this wonderful story called life.

With love,
Carlos Roldán Blay

I want to dedicate this book to my dad, Carlos Roldán Blay, PhD in Industrial Engineering, always eager to learn new things and with great love for his family: my mom, my brother, and me.

Dad, thank you for teaching me and sharing this exciting programming adventure with me. You are my inspiration and my guide at every step. I love learning with you, and I can't wait for us to embark on many more adventures together!

```
print("I love you, Dad!")
```

CONTENTS

ACKNOWLEDGMENTS

We want to express our deepest gratitude to everyone who has been a part of our journey and growth throughout our lives. To our teachers and mentors, who have guided and taught us with dedication and patience. To our friends and family, who have always supported us at every step of our learning and development.

A very special thank you to you, dear reader. Your interest in learning and having fun with this book motivates us and fills us with pride. We hope you enjoy this adventure as much as we enjoyed creating and sharing this knowledge with you. May this be just the beginning of your fascinating journey into the world of programming.

Thank you for joining us on this wonderful journey.

FOREWORD

Welcome to the world of programming with Python! This book has been created with love and dedication to help kids like you take their first steps into programming in a fun and accessible way.

Programming is an incredibly powerful skill that allows you to bring your ideas to life, solve problems, and create amazing things. With every line of code, you'll be building a solid foundation for your future in technology and innovation.

Throughout these chapters, I will guide you step by step through concepts and projects that will help you understand how Python works —one of the most popular and versatile programming languages in the world. You'll learn to create games, applications, and fun projects that will challenge your creativity and logic.

This book is not just a technical guide but also an invitation to explore, experiment, and, above all, enjoy the learning process. Together with my daughter Marta, we've designed this journey to be both educational and entertaining. Marta, with her curiosity and enthusiasm, has been an exceptional co-author and a constant source of inspiration.

By the end of this book, you will be equipped with the basic skills to continue exploring the vast universe of programming. Remember, this is just the beginning. Programming is an ongoing adventure, full of exciting discoveries and challenges.

Thank you for joining us on this journey. We're excited to see what you'll create and how you'll apply what you've learned. Let's embark on this incredible adventure together!

With enthusiasm and gratitude,

Carlos Roldán Blay and Marta Roldán Canti

CHAPTER 1: INTRODUCTION TO PROGRAMMING

1. What is Programming?

Hello, and welcome to the world of programming! But what is programming, exactly? Imagine you have a magical notebook where you can write instructions, and, as if by magic, your computer understands them and does exactly what you want. That's what programming is all about! It's a language that tells the computer what to do.

Programming is like having a superpower that lets you create your own games, apps, websites, and so much more. With programming, you can turn your ideas into reality and solve problems in creative ways.

2. Examples of Programming in Everyday Life

Programming is everywhere, and it's used in many things you see and use every day:

- **Video Games:** Do you like video games? Every game you play is made with programming. From the graphics to the game's logic, everything is created with code.
- **Apps:** The apps you use on your phone or tablet, like

games, calculators, and social media, are all made with programming.

- **Robots:** The robots you see in movies and TV shows —even the ones in real life— work thanks to programming.
- **Websites:** Every website you visit, from Google to YouTube, is built with programming.

3. What is Python?

Now that you know what programming is and how it's used in daily life, let's talk about Python. Python is a programming language that tells the computer what to do in a very simple and fun way.

3.1. Why Learn Python?

You might wonder, why should we learn Python? Here are a few reasons:

1. **Easy to Read and Write:** Python has a syntax (the way we write code) that's very similar to English. This makes it easy to read and understand.
2. **Versatile:** You can use Python to create games, apps, websites, data analysis, and so much more.
3. **Large Community:** Many people around the world use Python, which means you can always find help and resources online

4. Conclusion

Python is an excellent programming language to begin your adventure in coding. In the next chapter, we'll learn how to get ready to program by installing Python and a text editor, and we'll write our very first Python program!

CHAPTER 2: GETTING READY TO PROGRAM

1. Installing Python

To start programming in Python, we first need to install Python on our computer. If you already have an IDE (Integrated Development Environment) for Python, you can skip this section. Here's a simple guide for installing Python on different operating systems.

1.1. Windows

1. **Visit the Python website:** Go to python.org and download the latest version of Python.
   2. **Install Python:** Open the downloaded file and follow the instructions to install Python on your computer. Be sure to check the option "Add Python to PATH" during installation.

1.2. MacOS

1. **Visit the Python website:** Go to python.org and download the latest version of Python.
   2. **Install Python:** Open the downloaded file and follow the instructions to install Python on your computer.

1.3. Linux

1. Open a terminal.
    2. Type the following command to install Python:

```
sudo apt-get install python3
```

2. Installing a Text Editor (IDE)

An IDE is a program where you can write and run your code. There are several IDEs you can use to program in Python. Here are some recommendations:

- **Spyder:** An IDE specially designed for data scientists, included in the Anaconda environment. We like this one a lot, and it's what we've used for the examples in this book, but any other IDE should work just fine.
- **IDLE:** Comes included with the Python installation and is perfect for beginners.
- **Thonny:** A simple and easy-to-use IDE, ideal for those just starting out.
- **Mu:** Another simple IDE designed specifically to teach programming to kids.
- **PyCharm:** A very popular and powerful IDE for Python, with many advanced features.
- **VSCode (Visual Studio Code):** A highly versatile and customizable code editor with support for many programming languages.
- **Jupyter Notebook:** Ideal for writing and running code in blocks, commonly used in data science and education.

3. Hello, World

Let's start with something very simple but powerful. We're going to write our first Python program that says "Hello, World!"

3.1. Step 1: Open the Python Editor

Look for a program called "IDLE," "Thonny," "Spyder," or the editor you've chosen, and open it. This is the editor where we'll write and run our code. You might need to look up some tutorials online to get your first example working, but this is important because once you master this step, you'll be able to make the most of this book.

3.2. Step 2: Write the Code

Type the following code into the editor:

```
print("Hello, World!")
```

Code Example 1

3.3. Step 3: Run the Program

Save the file with a name like hello_world.py then select "Run" and "Run Module" from the menu. In some programs, this can also be done by pressing the F5 key. You'll see your program print "Hello, World!" on the screen. This screen is where the output of all the programs you create will appear.

Congratulations! You've written your first Python program.

Each code example in this book is a small program that you can write, edit to your liking, and save to try out later. By the end of this book, you could have a folder with over 100 small saved programs that you can open, run, or modify to create new programs with everything you've learned.

Let's take a look at a few screenshots of this example programmed in Spyder.

On the left panel, you'll see the code editor with the program we just created. I saved it in a folder where I'll keep all the programs I write while learning to program. This way, everything stays organized. I recommend you create a folder for everything you learn from this book. We run the program by clicking the green triangle button (Run) or pressing the F5 key.

On the other panel, you'll find the console, where the output of our programs is displayed when we run them. In line [1], we ran a program called `"001.py"` saved in the folder `E:/Python Book`. When we ran it, the output was: `Hello, World!`

4. Breaking Down Our First Program

Let's take a closer look at what our first program does. Each line gives a specific instruction to the computer.

- `print("Hello, World!")`: This line tells the computer that we want to display the text "Hello, World!" on the screen. The `print` function is one of the most basic and useful functions in Python. As you can see, what we want `print` to show on the screen is written inside parentheses. The phrase we want to display is enclosed in quotation marks. We'll explore all of this in more detail later on.

5. Experimenting with Python

Now that you've written your first program, let's have some more fun with Python. Here are some ideas to keep experimenting:

1. **Change the Message:** Change the text inside the quotation marks to say something else, like your name.

```
print("Hello, I'm [Your Name]!")
```
Code Example 2

Note: Replace `[Your Name]` with your name or another name to see what the program displays when you run it.

2. **Do Some Math:** Use Python like a calculator. Write the following commands in the editor and run them.

```
print(5 + 3)
print(10 - 2)
print(4 * 2)
print(16 / 2)
```
Code Example 3

> **Note**: Notice that this time we didn't use quotation marks. This means Python first interprets what you wrote (does the math) and then shows the result, instead of displaying the exact text you wrote.

3. **Combine Text and Numbers:** Try printing a message that mixes text and numbers.

```
print("I am", 10, "years old ")
```
Code Example 4

> **Note**: How does this message look? The first part is a word. The second part is a number that Python has to interpret. It could have been a math operation, like 8 + 2, instead of just a number. The third part is another word in quotation marks. Python will display all three parts on the screen, separated by spaces, in a single line.

6. Fun Exercises

Here are some exercises to practice what you've learned:

6.1. Exercise 1: Personal Introduction

Write a program that prints your name, your age, and your favorite hobby.

```
print("My name is [Your Name]")
print("I am [Your Age] years old")
print("I like [Your Hobby]")
```
Code Example 5

6.2. Exercise 2: Math Calculations

Write a program that performs and displays the results of the following math operations:

- Add 15 and 23
- Subtract 12 from 50
- Multiply 7 by 8
- Divide 144 by 12

```
print("15 + 23 =", 15 + 23)
print("50 - 12 =", 50 - 12)
print("7 * 8 =", 7 * 8)
print("144 / 12 =", 144 / 12)
```

Code Example 6

> **Note**: Can you see the difference between the first part of each line and the second? One is literal text, and the other is a calculation that Python interprets before showing the result.

6.3. Exercise 3: A Funny Phrase

Write a program that prints a funny phrase using multiple `print` lines.

```
print("Why did the computer go to the doctor?")
print("Because it caught a virus!")
```

Code Example 7

7. Ready for More Adventures?

Now that you've taken your first steps into the world of programming with Python, you're ready to explore even more. In the next chapters, we'll learn how to do increasingly exciting and challenging things. We'll create games, solve problems, and most importantly, have lots of fun!

Remember, the key to becoming a great programmer is practice and experimentation. Don't be afraid to make mistakes —they're part of the learning process! Every mistake teaches you something new and helps you become a better programmer.

Get ready for the next adventure in the world of Python! We'll discover how to use variables, make decisions in our code, and create amazing projects.

CHAPTER 3: BASIC PYTHON CONCEPTS

1. Python Syntax

The syntax of Python is the way we write programs so that the computer can understand them. Python is known for its simplicity and readability. Let's take a look at some basic elements of Python syntax. We can't cover everything here, but we'll try to add more details throughout the book so this introduction doesn't feel overwhelming. For now, let's focus on a few important points.

1.1. Whitespace

Imagine you're organizing your room. If everything is messy, it's hard to find what you need. Whitespace in Python is like keeping your room tidy. It helps the computer understand which parts of the code go together to form a block or a group of instructions.

In Python, whitespace (also called indentation) is very important. We use spaces or tabs (the TAB key on your keyboard) to group lines of code that belong to the same block or section of a program. For example, when we define a function or a loop, the code inside them must be indented.

- Example:

```
def greet():
```

```
print("Hello!")
print("How are you?")
```

Code Example 8

Important! This program doesn't do anything on its own. All we're doing is telling Python that we want to create a function called `greet`, and if someone runs it, it should display the two messages inside it. The important thing to notice is that there are lines of code written inside this function, all properly aligned and indented further to the right than the function definition itself.

In this example, the two lines that start with `print` are indented inside the function `greet()`. This tells Python that these two lines belong to the `greet` function.

Caution! In Python, not using the correct indentation can cause errors in your program. Always make sure that lines of code that belong together are properly aligned.

- Exercise:
1. Write a function called `say_goodbye` that prints "Goodbye!" and "See you later".
   2. Make sure the `print` lines are properly indented.
- Solution:

```
def say_goodbye():
    print("Goodbye!")
    print("See you later")
```

Code Example 9

2. Comments

Comments are lines of text that the program does not execute. We use them to explain the code and make notes. Think of comments like sticky notes you put in a book to remember important things.

In Python, comments start with the # symbol.

- Example:

```
# This is a comment
print("Hello, World!")  # This is also a comment
```

Code Example 10

Important! Comments are just for you. You can write notes in your programs that Python will ignore when running the code. This way, you can come back later, read them, and understand your own code better. If you place the # symbol at the beginning of a line, everything written after it on that line becomes a comment. Python will skip it when executing the program

Comments don't affect how the program works, but they are very helpful for explaining what your code does.

- Exercise:
1. Write a program that prints "Good morning!".
2. Add a comment at the beginning of the program that says, "This program prints a greeting".

- Solution:

```
# This program prints a greeting
print("Good morning!")
```
Code Example 11

3. Variables

Variables are like boxes where we store information. We can use variables to store numbers, text, and other types of data. Imagine each box has a label to help you know what's inside.

In Python, you don't need to declare the type of variable before using it. You simply assign a value to a variable name.

- Example:

```
age = 10
name = "Anna"
is_student = True
```
Code Example 12

In this example, age is a variable that stores the number 10, name stores the text "Anna" and is_student stores the value True (which means yes, right or true).

Try it yourself! Write a program where you declare a variable called my_favorite_color and assign it your favorite color. Then, print the value of this variable.

- Solution:

```
my_favorite_color = "Blue"
print(my_favorite_color)
```
Code Example 13

> **Important!** Why didn't we put quotation marks around `my_favorite_color` in the `print` statement? Because it's a variable, and we don't want Python to display its name literally. Instead, we want Python to interpret it —that is, to "open the box" and show the "contents," not the label. You can try adding another line to the program with quotation marks to see the difference: `print("my_favorite_color")`.

4. Data Types

Let's explore some basic data types that we can use in Python.

4.1. Numbers

Python can work with different types of numbers, like integers (`int`) (whole numbers) and floats (`float`) (numbers with decimals).

- Example:

```
integer = 5
floating_point = 5.5
```
Code Example 14

You can perform basic math operations with these numbers, like addition, subtraction, multiplication, and division.

- Example:

```
a = 10
b = 3
addition = a + b            # 13
subtraction = a - b         # 7
multiplication = a * b      # 30
division = a / b            # 3.333...
```
Code Example 15

> **Try it yourself!** Write a program that adds two numbers and displays the result.

- Solution:

```
number1 = 7
number2 = 5
result = number1 + number2
print(result)   # 12
```
Code Example 16

Did you know? You can use Python as a calculator to do your math homework. Try typing operations like 2 + 3 * 4 and see what result you get.

- More examples of math operations:

```
# Addition
addition = 8 + 2   # 10
print(addition)

# Subtraction
subtraction = 8 - 2   # 6
print(subtraction)

# Multiplication
multiplication = 8 * 2   # 16
print(multiplication)

# Division
division = 8 / 2   # 4.0
print(division)

# Floor division (no decimals)
floor_division = 8 // 3   # 2
print(floor_division)

# Modulus (remainder of division)
modulus = 8 % 3   # 2
print(modulus)
```
Code Example 17

Try this: Write a program that subtracts, multiplies, and divides two numbers of your choice, and displays the results.

4.2. Strings

Strings are sequences of characters (letters, numbers, and symbols) enclosed in single or double quotation marks. Think of them as a chain of letters that form words or sentences. These characters are letters, numbers, or other symbols, and they are ordered within the string starting from the first one (which is 0). In Python, counting starts at 0.

- Example:

```
message = "Hello, World"
name = 'Anna'
```
Code Example 18

You can combine (concatenate) strings using the + operator. Be careful —if one of the items is a number, you need to convert it to a string first by using str() and putting the value inside it. We'll explore examples of this later.

- Example:

```
name = 'Anna'
greeting = "Hello, " + name
print(greeting)  # Hello, Anna
```
Code Example 19

Try this! Write a program that takes your first name and last name and combines them into a single string.

- Solution:

```
first_name = "John"
last_name = "Doe"
full_name = first_name + " " + last_name
print(full_name)  # John Doe
```
Code Example 20

Tip: If you need to include quotation marks inside a string, you can use single and double quotes together. For example, "He said 'Hello'" or 'She said "Goodbye"'.

- Example:

```
sentence = "She said 'Hello'"
print(sentence)  # She said 'Hello'

sentence2 = 'He replied "Goodbye"'
print(sentence2)  # He replied "Goodbye"
```
Code Example 21

- String Methods:

Strings have methods that help us manipulate and work with text.

- Example:

```
text = "Python is fun!"
print(text.upper())  # PYTHON IS FUN!
print(text.lower())  # python is fun!
print(text.replace("fun", "awesome"))  # Python
is awesome!
```

Code Example 22

Try this: Write a program that converts a string to uppercase, then to lowercase, and finally replaces one word with another.

4.3. Lists

Lists are collections of items that are ordered and can be changed (modified). The elements in a list can be of different data types. Imagine a shopping list where you can add, remove, or change items.

- Example:

```
numbers = [1, 2, 3, 4, 5]
names = ["Anna", "Luis", "Carlos"]
mixed = [1, "two", 3.0, True]
```

Code Example 23

You can access items in a list using their index, which starts at 0.

Remember: In Python, counting starts at 0, not 1 as in some other languages.

- Example:

```
numbers = [1, 2, 3, 4, 5]
names = ["Anna", "Luis", "Carlos"]
first_number = numbers[0]  # 1
second_name = names[1]  # Luis
```

Code Example 24

You can add, remove, or change items in a list using methods like append, remove, and direct assignment.

- Example:

```
numbers = [1, 2, 3, 4, 5]
names = ["Anna", "Luis", "Carlos"]
mixed = [1, "two", 3.0, True]
numbers.append(6)  # Adds 6 to the end of the list
names.remove("Luis")   # Removes "Luis" from the
list
mixed[1] = "two"  # Changes the second element to
"two"
```
Code Example 25

Try it yourself! Create a list of your favorite foods and add a new food to the end.

- Solution:

```
favorite_foods  =  ["Pizza",  "Hamburger",  "Ice
Cream"]
favorite_foods.append("Sushi")
print(favorite_foods)  # ['Pizza', 'Hamburger',
'Ice Cream', 'Sushi']
```
Code Example 26

Did you know? Lists can contain other lists. This is called nested lists.

- Example:

```
nested_list = [[1, 2, 3], ["a", "b", "c"]]
print(nested_list[0])  # [1, 2, 3]
print(nested_list[1][1])  # b
```
Code Example 27

Note: In the second print, we access the variable nested_list, look for item 1 (the second list), which contains three letters, and display the second letter of that list.

- More examples with lists:

```
# Create a list
fruits = ["apple", "banana", "cherry"]
print(fruits)

# Access items
print(fruits[0])  # apple
```

```
print(fruits[2])  # cherry

# Change items
fruits[1] = "orange"
print(fruits)  # ['apple', 'orange', 'cherry']

# Remove items
fruits.remove("orange")
print(fruits)  # ['apple', 'cherry']

# Add items
fruits.append("grape")
print(fruits)  # ['apple', 'cherry', 'grape']

# Insert items in a specific position
fruits.insert(1, "pear")
print(fruits)  # ['apple', 'pear', 'cherry',
'grape']
```

Code Example 28

Try this: Write a program that creates a list of your favorite colors, changes one of the colors, removes another, and adds a new color to the end.

5. Final Exercise

Now it's your turn to practice everything you've learned in this chapter!

5.1. Task:

1. Create a variable to store your name.
2. Create a variable to store your age.
3. Create a list with three of your favorite colors.
4. Add another favorite color to the end of the list.
5. Print a message that says: "Hi, my name is [your name], I am [your age] years old! My favorite colors are [colors]."
   - Solution:

```
name = "YourName"
age = 10
favorite_colors = ["Red", "Green", "Blue"]
favorite_colors.append("Yellow")
print("Hi, my name is " + name + " and I am",
```

```
age, "years old! My favorite colors are",
favorite_colors, ".")
```

Code Example 29

In this code:

1. name is a word or text (also called a string in programming). Here it stores the name "YourName", or whatever name you write.
    2. age is a number. In this case, the age is 10.
    3. favorite_colors is a list, which is like a box where we store multiple favorite colors. At first, it contains "Red", "Green" and "Blue". Then we add "Yellow" using favorite_colors.append("Yellow"). In this example, all the list elements are strings (words), but this doesn't always have to be the case.

When we use print to display a message, we need to combine different types of data. In the message, we use a comma "," to separate the things we want to display:

```
print("Hi, my name is " + name + " and I am",
age, "years old! My favorite colors are",
favorite_colors, ".")
```

Here we use the comma because:

- name is a string, and we can easily combine it with other strings using the + sign.
- age is a number. Numbers can't be combined directly with text using +, so we separate it with a comma ",". The comma tells Python to display the value of the age variable as it is.
- favorite_colors is a list, and it is also displayed using a comma ",".

Another way to do this is to convert the numbers and lists to text using str(). This way, we can combine everything with +:

```
print("Hi, my name is " + name + " and I am " +
str(age) + " years old! My favorite colors are "
+ str(favorite_colors) + ".")
```

Here:

- str(age) converts the number stored in the age

variable to text.

- `str(favorite_colors)` converts the list of colors to text.

This allows us to combine everything using the + sign. And that's it! This is how we can display messages with different types of data in Python.

6. Additional Exercises

To strengthen what you've learned, here are some extra exercises. Try solving them without looking at the solutions first.

6.1. Exercise 1:

1. Create a variable to store the name of your pet.
    2. Create a variable to store the age of your pet.
    3. Print a message that says: " My pet's name is [pet's name], and it is [pet's age] years old."
    - Solution:

```
pet_name = "Fido"
pet_age = 3
print("My pet's name is " + pet_name + " and it
is " + str(pet_age) + " years old.")
```

Code Example 30

6.2. Exercise 2:

1. Create a list with the names of three of your friends.
2. Change the second name in the list to another name.
3. Remove the first name from the list.
4. Add a new name to the end of the list.
5. Print the resulting list.
    - Solution:

```
friends = ["James", "Emily", "Oliver"]
friends[1] = "Sophia"
friends.remove("James")
friends.append("Liam")
print(friends)  # ['Sophia', 'Oliver', 'Liam']
```

Code Example 31

6.3. Exercise 3:

1. Create a string that says: "I like programming in Python."
2. Convert the entire string to uppercase and display it.
3. Convert the entire string to lowercase and display it.
4. Replace the word "Python" with "JavaScript" and display the new string.
   - Solution:

```
text = "I like programming in Python"
print(text.upper())  # I LIKE PROGRAMMING IN PYTHON
print(text.lower())  # i like programming in python
new_text = text.replace("Python", "JavaScript")
print(new_text)  # I like programming in JavaScript
```

Code Example 32

6.4. Exercise 4:

1. Create a list with five numbers.
2. Calculate the sum of all the numbers in the list.
3. Calculate the average of the numbers in the list.
4. Print the sum and the average.
   - Solution:

```
numbers = [4, 7, 1, 8, 3]
total = sum(numbers)
average = total / len(numbers)
print("Sum:", total)  # Sum: 23
print("Average:", average)  # Average: 4.6
```

Code Example 33

If you don't know what the average or `len` is, don't worry — these exercises are meant to introduce new concepts. The average of five numbers is their sum divided by 5. To show how `sum` and `len` work: `sum(list)` calculates the total of the numbers in a list and `len(list)` counts how many numbers are in the list. These concepts are a bit more advanced, but you'll get used to them with practice.

6.5. Wrapping Up

In this chapter, we've learned about Python syntax, comments, variables, and basic data types. We've explored some examples that challenge our imagination and creativity. With these fundamentals, you can now start writing more complex and useful programs. Keep going —you're doing great!

CHAPTER 4: DATA TYPES

1. Numbers

Python can work with different types of numbers. The two most common types are:

- Integers (`int`): Numbers without decimals.
- Floats (`float`): Numbers with decimals.

Note: This is interesting but important. In Python, 1 is an integer, while 1.0 is a float. They are not the same, even though they are mathematically equal.

1.1. Integers

Integers are numbers without decimals. They can be positive, negative, or zero. They can also be quite large, but not infinite — this might be important in the future. For now, let's focus on the fact that they don't have decimals.

- Example:

```
positive_number = 5
negative_number = -3
zero = 0
```

Code Example 34

You can perform math operations with integers, like addition, subtraction, multiplication, and division.

- Example:

```
a = 10
b = 3
addition = a + b          # 13
subtraction = a - b       # 7
multiplication = a * b    # 30
division = a / b          # 3.333... This is a
float
```
Code Example 35

- Exercise:
1. Declare two variables with integer numbers.
2. Perform addition, subtraction, multiplication, and division with these variables.
3. Print the results.
   - Solution:

```
number1 = 8
number2 = 2
addition = number1 + number2
subtraction = number1 - number2
multiplication = number1 * number2
division = number1 / number2
print("Addition:", addition)        # Addition: 10
print("Subtraction:", subtraction)  # Subtraction:
6
print("Multiplication:",   multiplication)        #
Multiplication: 16
print("Division:", division)        # Division:
4.0
```
Code Example 36

1.2. Floats

Floats are numbers with decimals. They can also be positive, negative, or zero.

- Example:

```
positive_number = 5.7
negative_number = -3.4
zero = 0.0
```
Code Example 37

Python for Little Geniuses: Discover Programming

Just like integers, we can perform math operations with floats.

- Example:

```
a = 5.5
b = 2.2
addition = a + b            # 7.7
subtraction = a - b         # 3.3
multiplication = a * b      # 12.1
division = a / b            # 2.5
```
Code Example 38

- Exercise:
1. Declare two variables with float numbers.
2. Perform addition, subtraction, multiplication, and division with these variables.
3. Print the results.

- Solution:

```
number1 = 3.6
number2 = 1.2
addition = number1 + number2
subtraction = number1 - number2
multiplication = number1 * number2
division = number1 / number2
print("Addition:", addition)          # Addition: 4.8
print("Subtraction:", subtraction)  # Subtraction:
2.4
print("Multiplication:",   multiplication)      #
Multiplication: 4.32
print("Division:", division)          # Division:
3.0
```
Code Example 39

2. Strings

As we've seen before, strings are sequences of characters (letters, numbers, and symbols) enclosed in single or double quotes. Strings are mainly used to store text. It's important to practice with strings because they're incredibly useful in programming.

- Example:

```
message = "Hello, World"
```

25

```
name = 'Anna'
```
Code Example 40

You can combine (concatenate) strings using the + operator.

- Example:

```
message = "Hello, World"
name = 'Anna'
greeting = "Hello, " + name
print(greeting)  # Hello, Anna
```
Code Example 41

You can also repeat strings using the * operator.

- Example:

```
repeat = "Hooray! " * 3
print(repeat)  # Hooray! Hooray! Hooray!
```
Code Example 42

Note: Here, the variable `repeat` contains the exclamation, followed by the letters "H," "o," "o," "r," "a," "y," an exclamation mark, and a space, repeated three times.

- Exercise:
1. Declare a variable with your name.
2. Declare another variable with your favorite greeting.
3. Combine these two variables into a single message and repeat the greeting three times.
4. Print the resulting message.

- Solution:

```
name = "John"
greeting = "Good morning!"
message = (greeting + " " + name + " ") * 3
print(message)  # Good morning! John Good
morning! John Good morning! John
```
Code Example 43

2.1. String Methods

Strings have methods that help us manipulate and work with text. Here are some common methods, including a few we've already seen:

- `.upper()`: Converts the string to uppercase.

26

- `.lower()`: Converts the string to lowercase.
- `.replace("old", "new")`: Replaces part of the string with another string.
- `.find("substring")`: Finds the position of a substring within a string.
- Example:

```
text = "Python is fun!"
print(text.upper())  # PYTHON IS FUN!
print(text.lower())  # python is fun!
print(text.replace("fun", "awesome"))  # Python is
awesome!
print(text.find("Python"))  # 0
```
Code Example 44

- Exercise:
1. Declare a variable with some text you like.
2. Convert the text to uppercase and lowercase.
3. Replace a word in the text with another word.
4. Find the position of a word in the text.
5. Print the results.
- Solution:

```
text = "I love programming in Python"
print(text.upper())  # I LOVE PROGRAMMING IN PYTHON
print(text.lower())  # i love programming in python
new_text = text.replace("Python", "JavaScript")
print(new_text)  # I love programming in JavaScript
position = text.find("programming")
print(position)  # 7
```
Code Example 45

Remember: The first character of the text is at position 0, the second is at position 1, and so on. That's why the position of "programming" is 7 —because that's where the word starts if you count from 0, including spaces.

3. Lists

Lists are collections of items that are ordered and can be changed (modified). The elements in a list can be of different data types. Imagine a shopping list where you can add, remove, or change items.

- Example:

```
numbers = [1, 2, 3, 4, 5]
names = ["Anna", "James", "Oliver"]
mixed = [1, "two", 3.0, True]
```
Code Example 46

You can access the elements of a list using indexes, which start at 0.

- Example:

```
numbers = [1, 2, 3, 4, 5]
names = ["Anna", "James", "Oliver"]
first_number = numbers[0]  # 1
second_name = names[1]  # James
```
Code Example 47

You can add, remove, or change elements in a list using methods like append, remove, and direct assignment, which is very useful.

- Example:

```
numbers = [1, 2, 3, 4, 5]
names = ["Anna", "James", "Oliver"]
mixed = [1, "two", 3.0, True]
numbers.append(6)      # Adds 6 to the end of the
list
names.remove("James")  # Removes "James" from the
list
mixed[1] = "two"       # Changes the second
element to "two"
```
Code Example 48

- Exercise:
1. Create a list of your favorite fruits.
2. Add a new fruit to the end of the list.
3. Change one fruit in the list to another fruit.
4. Remove a fruit from the list.
5. Print the resulting list.
   - Solution:

```
fruits = ["apple", "banana", "cherry"]
```

```
fruits.append("pear")    # Add a new fruit
fruits[1] = "orange"     # Change banana to orange
fruits.remove("cherry")  # Remove cherry
print(fruits)  # ['apple', 'orange', 'pear']
```

Code Example 49

Did you know? Lists can contain other lists. This is called nested lists. In that case, the elements of a list are other lists, and the elements of those lists can be anything (numbers, strings, lists, etc.).

- Example:

```
nested_list = [[1, 2, 3], ["a", "b", "c"]]
print(nested_list[0])  # [1, 2, 3]
print(nested_list[1][1])  # b
```

Code Example 50

- More List Examples:

```
# Create a list
colors = ["red", "green", "blue"]
print(colors)

# Access elements
print(colors[0])  # red
print(colors[2])  # blue

# Change elements
colors[1] = "yellow"
print(colors)  # ['red', 'yellow', 'blue']

# Remove elements
colors.remove("red")
print(colors)  # ['yellow', 'blue']

# Add elements
colors.append("purple")
print(colors)  # ['yellow', 'blue', 'purple']

# Insert elements at a specific position
colors.insert(1, "orange")
print(colors)  # ['yellow', 'orange', 'blue',
'purple']
```

Code Example 51

Try this: Write a program that creates a list of your

29

favorite animals, changes one of the animals, removes another, and adds a new animal to the end.

4. Final Exercise

Now it's your turn to put into practice everything you've learned in this chapter!

4.1. Task:

1. Create a variable to store your name.
2. Create a variable to store your age.
3. Create a list with three of your favorite colors.
4. Add another favorite color to the end of the list.
5. Print a message that says" Hi, my name is [your name], and I am [your age] years old! My favorite colors are [colors]."

   • Solution:

```
name = "YourName"
age = 10
favorite_colors = ["Red", "Green", "Blue"]
favorite_colors.append("Yellow")
print("Hi, my name is " + name + " and I am " +
str(age) + " years old! My favorite colors are "
+ str(favorite_colors) + ".")
```

Code Example 52

5. Additional Exercises

To strengthen what you've learned, here are some extra exercises. Try solving them without looking at the solutions first. However, the solutions are provided so you can repeat them and try to understand as much as possible. Remember, this is just the beginning!

5.1. Exercise 1:

1. Create a variable to store the name of your pet.
2. Create a variable to store the age of your pet.
3. Print a message that says: " My pet's name is [pet's name], and it is [pet's age] years old."

   • Solution:

```
pet_name = "Fido"
pet_age = 3
print("My pet's name is " + pet_name + " and it
is " + str(pet_age) + " years old.")
```
Code Example 53

5.2. Exercise 2:

1. Create a list with the names of three of your friends.
2. Change the second name in the list to another name of your choice.
3. Remove the first name from the list.
4. Add a new name to the end of the list.
5. Print the resulting list.
   - Solution:

```
friends = ["James", "Emily", "Oliver"]
friends[1] = "Sophia"
friends.remove("James")
friends.append("Liam")
print(friends)  # ['Sophia', 'Oliver', 'Liam']
```
Code Example 54

5.3. Exercise 3:

1. Create a string that says: "I like programming in Python".
2. Convert the entire string to uppercase and display it.
3. Convert the entire string to lowercase and display it.
4. Replace the word "Python" with "JavaScript" and display the new string.
   - Solution:

```
text = "I like programming in Python"
print(text.upper())  # I LIKE PROGRAMMING IN PYTHON
print(text.lower())  # i like programming in python
new_text = text.replace("Python", "JavaScript")
print(new_text)  # I like programming in
JavaScript
```
Code Example 55

5.4. Exercise 4:

1. Create a list with five numbers.
2. Calculate the sum of all the numbers in the list using the built-in `sum` function in Python.
3. Calculate the average of the numbers in the list. This is done by dividing the sum by the number of items, which can be calculated using the `len` function.
4. Print the sum and the average.

   - Solution:

```
numbers = [4, 7, 1, 8, 3]
total = sum(numbers)
average = total / len(numbers)
print("Sum:", total)  # Sum: 23
print("Average:", average)  # Average: 4.6
```
Code Example 56

> **Tip:** Python provides many built-in functions, such as `sum` (to calculate the total) and `len` (to count items in a list), which make programming easier and more efficient. However, you can repeat the exercise without these functions using the following alternative solution. Later, we'll learn how to use loops to iterate through the elements of a list to perform operations like summing or counting them.

   - Alternative solution:

```
numbers = [4, 7, 1, 8, 3]
total = numbers[0] + numbers[1] + numbers[2] +
numbers[3] + numbers[4]
count = 5
average = total / count
print("Sum:", total)  # Sum: 23
print("Average:", average)  # Average: 4.6
```
Code Example 57

5.5. Wrapping Up

In this chapter, we've learned about the different data types in Python, how to work with them, and how to perform basic operations. With this knowledge, you're now ready to start creating more complex and useful programs. Keep going and enjoy programming!

CHAPTER 5: CONTROL FLOW AND DATA INPUT

1. Control Flow

Control flow in Python allows us to make decisions in our programs and repeat certain actions. The two most important concepts in control flow are conditionals and loops.

1.1. Conditionals

Conditionals let us make decisions in our program. We use the `if`, `elif`, and `else` statements to execute different blocks of code based on certain conditions. It's similar to real life: *if this happens, we'll do this thing; if not, then we'll do something else.*

1.2. What are Conditionals?

Imagine you're playing a game where you have to decide whether to cross a river.

- **If** there's a bridge, you can cross.
- **If** there's no bridge, but there's a boat, you can also cross.
- **Otherwise**, if there's neither a bridge nor a boat, you can't cross.

This is similar to how conditionals work in programming!

1.3. Syntax of Conditionals

The basic structure of a conditional in Python is as follows:

```
if condition:
    # Code block if the condition is true
elif another_condition:
    # Code block if the other condition is true
else:
    # Code block if no condition is true
```

- Example:

```
age = 18
if age >= 18:
    print("You are an adult.")
else:
    print("You are a minor.")
```
Code Example 58

Try it out: Run this program and change the age to different values, either less than 18 or greater than 18, to check that the conditional works as expected.

In this example, if the variable age is greater than or equal to 18, it prints "You are an adult." Otherwise, it prints "You are a minor."

Analogy: Think of a conditional as a fork in the road. Depending on whether a condition is true or false, you'll take one path or another.

- More Examples of Conditionals:

```
# Using elif
day = "Monday"
if day == "Monday":
    print("It's Monday, the week is starting.")
elif day == "Friday":
    print("It's Friday, almost the weekend!")
else:
    print("It's another day of the week.")
```
Code Example 59

Note: The comparison operators we use in conditionals are:

== equal to

> != not equal to
> \> greater than
> < less than
> >= greater than or equal to
> <= less than or equal to

- Exercise:
1. Declare a variable `temperature` and assign it a value.
2. Write a conditional that prints:
   - "It's cold" if the temperature is less than 15 degrees.
   - "It's hot" if it's greater than 25 degrees.
   - "The weather is pleasant" for other values.
3. Print the result.
   - Solution:

```
temperature = 20
if temperature < 15:
    print("It's cold")
elif temperature > 25:
    print("It's hot")
else:
    print("The weather is pleasant")
```

Code Example 60

1.4. Loops

Loops allow us to repeat actions multiple times. In Python, there are two main types of loops: `for` and `while`. These words translate to "for" and "while." Think of it like this: *"do this 10 times in a row"* or *"do this while it's not dinnertime"*.

1.5. The `for` loop

The `for` loop is used to iterate over a sequence (like a list or a string). Imagine you have a pack of cookies and you want to eat one cookie at a time until the pack is empty. The `for` loop does something similar —it repeats an action for every item in a sequence.

1.6. Syntax of the `for` loop

```
for variable in sequence:
    # Code block executed in each iteration
```

- Example:

```
for number in [1, 2, 3, 4, 5]:
    print(number)
```

Code Example 61

Explanation: This program takes each number from the list and starts running the loop. First, it takes 1 and calls it number, then it executes print(number). Next, it takes 2, calls it number, and executes print(number) again. In other words, number is a variable that takes a different value from the list [1, 2, 3, 4, 5] in each iteration of the for loop.

- More Examples of for Loops:

```
# Iterating over a string
for letter in "Python":
    print(letter)

# Using range() to iterate over a sequence of
numbers
for i in range(5):
    print(i)
```

Code Example 62

Tips: A string is like a list of letters, so the for loop works with it too. The range function generates numbers starting from 0 up to (but not including) the number you provide.

- Exercise:

1. Create a list of your three favorite fruits.
2. Use a for loop to print each fruit in the list.

- Solution:

```
fruits = ["apple", "banana", "cherry"]
for fruit in fruits:
    print(fruit)
```

Code Example 63

1.7. The while loop

The while loop repeats a block of code as long as a condition is true. It's like saying: *"While there are cookies in the pack, keep eating"*.

1.8. Syntax of the `while` loop

```
while condition:
    # Code block executed while the condition is
true
```

- Example:

```
counter = 0
while counter < 5:
    print(counter)
    counter = counter + 1
```

Code Example 64

> **Tip:** You can write `counter += 1` instead of `counter = counter + 1` —this is a shorter way to say the same thing. Python has many ways to make your code more compact!

In this example, the `while` loop prints the value of `counter` as long as `counter` is less than 5. After each iteration, `counter` increases by 1.

- Exercise:
1. Use a `while` loop to print the numbers from 1 to 5.
- Solution:

```
counter = 1
while counter <= 5:
    print(counter)
    counter += 1
```

Code Example 65

> **Important!** If you forget to write `counter += 1` inside the `while` loop, the program won't know when to stop. That's because `counter` would never change and would always stay at 1, which is less than or equal to 5, causing the loop to repeat endlessly. This is called an **infinite loop**. Yikes! To avoid this, always make sure the `counter` or any variable you use in the loop changes somehow so the loop can end. That's how the `while` loop works and why it's important to ensure the `counter` updates in each iteration.

2. Getting User Input with `input`

The `input` function lets us ask the user for information. This function pauses the program and waits for the user to enter a value. The value entered is always stored as a string.

- Example:

```
name = input("What's your name? ")
print("Hello, " + name + "!")
```

Code Example 66

In this example, the program asks the user for their name and then prints a personalized greeting. When you run it, the program displays the question, and the user must type their answer and press Enter for the program to continue.

> **Note:** If you need the user to enter a number, you must convert the text input to a number using `int()` or `float()`.

- Example:

```
age = int(input("How old are you? "))
print("You will be " + str(age + 1) + " years old
next year.")
```

Code Example 67

In this example, the program asks the user for their age, converts it to an integer, and then calculates how old they'll be next year.

- Exercise:
1. Ask the user to enter their name.
2. Ask the user to enter their age.
3. Print a message that says: *"Hello, [name]. You are [age] years old."*

- Solution:

```
name = input("What's your name? ")
age = int(input("How old are you? "))
print("Hello, " + name + ". You are " + str(age)
+ " years old.")
```

Code Example 68

- Exercise 2:
1. Ask the user to enter a number.

Python for Little Geniuses: Discover Programming

2. Use a `for` loop to print all the numbers from 1 up to the entered number.
   • Solution:

```
number = int(input("Enter a number: "))
for i in range(1, number + 1):
    print(i)
```
Code Example 69

3. Additional Exercises

To reinforce what you've learned, here are some extra exercises. Try solving them without looking at the solutions first!

3.1. Exercise 1:

1. Ask the user to enter their favorite food.
2. Use a `for` loop to print their favorite food three times.
   • Solution:

```
favorite_food = input("What's your favorite food? ")
for i in range(3):
    print(favorite_food)
```
Code Example 70

3.2. Exercise 2:

1. Ask the user to enter a number.
2. Use a `while` loop to print the numbers from 1 to the entered number.
   • Solution:

```
number = int(input("Enter a number: "))
counter = 1
while counter <= number:
    print(counter)
    counter += 1
```
Code Example 71

3.3. Exercise 3:

1. Ask the user to enter their name.

39

2. Ask the user to enter the number of repetitions.
3. Use a `for` loop to print the user's name the specified number of times.
   • Solution:

```
name = input("What's your name? ")
repetitions = int(input("How many times do you want
to see your name? "))
for i in range(repetitions):
    print(name)
```

Code Example 72

3.4. Exercise 4:

1. Ask the user to enter two numbers.
2. Use a conditional to determine which number is larger, which is smaller, or if they are equal.
3. Print a message indicating the result.
   • Solution:

```
number1 = int(input("Enter the first number: "))
number2 = int(input("Enter the second number: "))
if number1 > number2:
    print(str(number1) + " is greater than " +
str(number2))
elif number1 < number2:
    print(str(number1) + " is smaller than " +
str(number2))
else:
    print(str(number1) + " is equal to " +
str(number2))
```

Code Example 73

Note: You can convert numeric variables into text using the `str` function that already exists in Python. This allows you to combine all phrases using the + symbol. Let's look at another way to do this.

   • Alternative solution:

```
number1 = int(input("Enter the first number: "))
number2 = int(input("Enter the second number: "))
if number1 > number2:
    print(number1, "is greater than", number2)
```

```
elif number1 < number2:
    print(number1, "is smaller than", number2)
else:
    print(number1, "is equal to", number2)
```

Code Example 74

3.5. Exercise 5:

1. Ask the user to enter a word.
2. Use a `for` loop to print each letter of the word on a separate line.

   • Solution:

```
word = input("Enter a word: ")
for letter in word:
    print(letter)
```

Code Example 75

In this chapter, we've explored how to control the flow of our programs and how to interact with the user through data input. You've learned to make decisions using conditionals, repeat actions with loops, and make your programs more dynamic with the `input` function. With these tools, you have the power to make your programs think, react, and adapt to different situations. Now you're ready to take on more exciting challenges and keep creating unique projects! Keep coding and let your imagination soar! 🚀

CHAPTER 6: FUNCTIONS IN PYTHON

1. What is a Function?

A function is like a recipe. Imagine you want to make a pizza. You need to follow a series of steps: prepare the dough, add the toppings, and bake it. In programming, a function is a set of instructions we follow to accomplish something specific, just like a pizza recipe.

2. Why Use Functions?

Functions are useful because:
- They help us avoid repeating the same code.
- They make the code easier to read and understand.
- They allow us to break a big problem into smaller, more manageable parts.

3. Defining a Function

To define a function in Python, we use the keyword `def`, followed by the function name and parentheses `()`. Inside the parentheses, we can include parameters that the function needs to work. Then, we write an indented block of code that makes up the body of the function.

3.1. Syntax

```
def function_name(parameters):
    # Code block
```

- Let's look at an example that might sound familiar (a trip down memory lane):

```
def greet():
    print("Hello!")
    print("How are you?")
```

Code Example 76

In this example, we've defined a function called `greet` that prints two lines of text. By itself, this code doesn't produce any visible result —we're just defining the function so it can be used later.

4. Calling a Function

To use a function, simply write its name followed by parentheses `()`. This is called "calling" the function.

- Example:

```
def greet():
    print("Hello!")
    print("How are you?")

greet()
```

Code Example 77

In this example, we define the function `greet` and then call it, which makes the block of code inside the function execute.

5. Parameters and Arguments

Functions can receive information through parameters. Parameters are like the ingredients in a recipe. Arguments are the actual values we pass to the function when we call it. We can either pass a variable to the function, so it uses the variable's value, or directly pass a value for it to use when it runs.

- Example:

```
def greet(name):
    print("Hello, " + name + "!")
    print("How are you?")

greet("Anna")
greet("James")
```

Code Example 78

In this example, the function `greet` has a parameter called name. When we call the function (run it), we pass the arguments `"Anna"` and `"James"`, which are then used inside the function.

6. Breaking Down an Example

Let's look at an example step by step to better understand how functions with parameters work.

6.1. Step-by-Step Example

```
def greet(name):
    print("Hello, " + name + "!")
    print("How are you?")

greet("Anna")
```

Code Example 79

1. Function Definition:

```
def greet(name):
```

Here we're defining a function called `greet` that has a parameter named name.

2. Function Body:

```
    print("Hello, " + name + "!")
    print("How are you?")
```

This is the block of code that will run when we call the function. It prints a personalized greeting using the value of the parameter name. Notice that this block of code is indented, with spaces added before each line so that everything aligns properly. This tells Python that these lines are part of the function definition.

3. Function Call:

```
greet("Anna")
```

Here we're calling the `greet` function and passing it the argument `"Anna"`. The function will use this value for the `name` parameter.

4. **Function Execution:**

When we call `greet("Anna")`, the output will be:

```
Hello, Anna!
How are you?
```

5. **Understanding the Order of Execution**

It's important to understand the order in which this code runs. Normally, a program executes from the first line to the last, in order. We've seen how conditionals and loops can alter this flow. Functions also change the flow of the program because the program "jumps" to the function when it's called, executes its code, and then returns to continue where it left off. Let's analyze this!

6.2. Step-by-Step Example Analysis

First, let's remember what a function is. A function is like a small recipe or a set of instructions we give to the computer to do something specific when we ask it to.

1. **Create the Function:**

```
def greet(name):
    print("Hello, " + name + "!")
    print("How are you?")
```

- `def greet(name):` This line says, "I'm creating a recipe called `greet` that needs an ingredient called name". Note that this line ends with ":".
- `print("Hello, " + name + "!")`: This line is one of the instructions in the recipe. It says, "Print (show on the screen) `Hello, name!`".
- `print("How are you?")`: This line is another instruction in the recipe. It says, "Print `How are you?`".

2. **Use the Function:**

```
greet("Anna")
```

- This line says, "Use the recipe greet and give it the ingredient Anna".

6.3. Order of Execution

How does the code run?
1. **First**, the program reads the first three lines:

```
def greet(name):
    print("Hello, " + name + "!")
    print("How are you?")
```

The program understands that we've created a recipe (function) called greet, but it doesn't do anything with it yet. It just remembers it and saves it in memory to use later. Think of it like writing down a recipe for future use.

2. **Next**, the program reaches the last line:

```
greet("Anna")
```

Here, the program says: "Ah, now I need to use the greet recipe with the ingredient Anna".

3. **Then**, the program goes to the recipe (the greet function) and follows the instructions inside it:

print("Hello, " + name + "!"): Displays on the screen "Hello, Anna!".

print("How are you?"): Displays on the screen "How are you?".

4. **Finally**, after using the recipe (running the function), the program continues with anything else that comes after it (if there are more lines of code).

In Summary:

- **Creating the function** is like writing a recipe.
- **Using the function** is like following the recipe to do something (in this case, greeting Anna).
- The program reads and saves the recipe first, but it only uses it when told to, with the ingredients we provide. You can use it as many times as you want, but you only need to define it once at the beginning.

7. Returning Values

Functions can return a value using the `return` keyword. This is useful when we want the function to perform a calculation and give us the result.

- Example:

```
def add(a, b):
    return a + b

result = add(3, 4)
print("The result is:", result)
```
Code Example 80

In this example, the `add` function takes two parameters, a and b, and returns their sum. Then, we call the function with the arguments 3 and 4 and store the result in the variable `result`.

> **Tip:** Notice these words: function, parameters, and arguments. These terms are often used in programming, and you'll get more familiar with them as you practice.

8. Breaking Down an Example with `return`

Let's look at an example step by step to better understand how functions that return values work.

8.1. Step-by-Step Example

```
def multiply(a, b):
    return a * b

result = multiply(6, 7)
print("The result is:", result)
```
Code Example 81

1. **Function Definition:**

```
def multiply(a, b):
```
Here, we're defining a function called `multiply` that has two parameters, a and b.

2. **Function Body:**

```
return a * b
```

> **Note:** This is the block of code that runs when we call the function. It calculates the product of a and b and returns the result. Notice that we don't write `return "a * b"` because we want Python to calculate a * b and return the result, not the phrase `"a * b"`.

3. **Function Call:**

```
result = multiply(6, 7)
```

Here, we're calling the `multiply` function and passing it the arguments 6 and 7. The function calculates 6 * 7 and returns 42, which is stored in the variable `result`.

4. **Printing the Result:**

```
print("The result is:", result)
```

The output will be:

```
The result is: 42
```

9. Final Exercise

Now it's your turn to put into practice everything you've learned in this chapter! Let's work on a task using everything we've covered.

9.1. Task

1. Create a function called `divide` that takes two parameters and returns their quotient.
2. Call the function with the arguments 20 and 4.
3. Print the result.
   - Solution:

```
def divide(a, b):
    return a / b

result = divide(20, 4)
print("The result is:", result)
```

Code Example 82

10. Additional Exercises

To reinforce what you've learned, here are some extra exercises. Try solving them without looking at the solutions first!

10.1. Exercise 1

1. Create a function called `greet_person` that takes a parameter `name` and prints `"Hello, [name]"`.
2. Call the function with your own name.
   - Solution:

```
def greet_person(name):
    print("Hello, " + name)

greet_person("John")
```

Code Example 83

10.2. Exercise 2

1. Create a function called `square` that takes a number and returns its square (the number multiplied by itself).
2. Call the function with the number 5 and store the result in a variable.
3. Print the result.
   - Solution:

```
def square(number):
    return number ** 2

result = square(5)
print("The result is:", result)
```

Code Example 84

Note: Here, we used `number ** 2` to calculate the square, but you could also write `number * number`.

10.3. Exercise 3

1. Create a function called `is_even` that takes a number and returns `True` if the number is even, and `False` if it's odd.
2. Call the function with the number 4 and store the result in a variable.
3. Print the result.

- Solution:

```
def is_even(number):
    if number % 2 == 0:
        is_even_or_not = True  # Assign True if the
number is even
    else:
        is_even_or_not = False  # Assign False if
the number is odd
    return is_even_or_not  # Return the result

result = is_even(4)
print("The number is even:", result)
```
Code Example 85

Would you like to see a more compact solution? It's not necessary to store `True` or `False` in a variable; we can use `return` directly within each condition. Check out this alternative:

```
def is_even(number):
    if number % 2 == 0:
        return True
    else:
        return False

result = is_even(4)
print("The number is even:", result)
```
Code Example 86

Would you like to see an even more compact solution? It's not necessary to use an `if` statement, as the result of the comparison will already be exactly `True` or `False`. Take a look at this new alternative:

```
def is_even(number):
    return number % 2 == 0

result = is_even(4)
print("The number is even:", result)
```
Code Example 87

Tip: In Python, it's common to find ways to write code in a very compact and efficient manner, making it both interesting and convenient.

10.4. Exercise 4

1. Create a function called `calculate_circle_area` that takes the radius of a circle and returns its area. (Area = π * radius * radius, use `3.14` as the value for π, a number called pi).
2. Call the function with a radius of `3` and store the result in a variable.
3. Print the result.
   - Solution:

```
def calculate_circle_area(radius):
    pi = 3.14
    return pi * radius * radius

result = calculate_circle_area(3)
print("The area of the circle is:", result)
```

Code Example 88

10.5. Exercise 5

1. Create a function called `calculate_average` that takes a list of numbers and returns their average (if you're unsure what this is, just check the solution).
2. Call the function with the list `[10, 20, 30, 40, 50]` and store the result in a variable.
3. Print the result.
   - Solution:

```
def calculate_average(numbers):
    total = sum(numbers)
    count = len(numbers)
    return total / count

result = calculate_average([10, 20, 30, 40, 50])
print("The average is:", result)
```

Code Example 89

10.6. Exercise 6

1. Create a function called `personalized_greeting` that takes two arguments: a `name` and an `age`.

2. The function should print a message saying: "Hello, [name]! You are [age] years old."
3. Call the function with the name "Anthony" and the age 12.

 • Solution:

```
def personalized_greeting(name, age):
    print("Hello, " + name + "! You are " + str(age)
+ " years old.")

# Call the function with the name "Anthony" and age
12
personalized_greeting("Anthony", 12)
```
Code Example 90

Note: As you can see, a function can have multiple arguments.

10.7. Wrapping Up

In this chapter, we've learned about functions in Python: what they are, why they're useful, how to define them, how to call them, how to pass parameters, and how to return values. With this knowledge, you can now create more organized and reusable programs. Keep going and enjoy the journey of programming!

CHAPTER 7: FUN PROJECTS

In this chapter, we'll create some fun projects using Python. These projects will help you practice everything you've learned so far about variables, data types, control flow, functions, and data input.

1. Project 1: Guessing Game

We'll create a simple guessing game where the computer selects a random number, and the player has to guess it.

1.1. Step 1: Import the `random` Library

Python has a library called `random` that allows us to generate random numbers. To use it, we first need to import it.

```
import random
```

1.2. Step 2: Define the Main Game Function

We'll define a function called `guessing_game` that will contain all the logic for the game.

```
def guessing_game():
    secret_number = random.randint(1, 100)    #
Choose a random number between 1 and 100
    attempts = 0
    guessed = False
```

```
    print("Welcome to the Guessing Game!")
    print("I'm thinking of a number between 1 and
100.")

    while not guessed:
        guess = int(input("Guess the number: "))
        attempts += 1

        if guess == secret_number:
            print(f"Congratulations!  You  guessed
the number in {attempts} attempts.")
            guessed = True
        elif guess < secret_number:
            print("The number is higher.")
        else:
            print("The number is lower.")
```

Note: We've used an **f-string** to make the `print` statement more dynamic. Instead of writing: `" Congratulations! You guessed the number in " + str(attempts) + " attempts."`, we add an f before the string and use curly braces `{attempts}` inside the text to substitute it with the value of the variable. It's a handy feature to know, but if it feels strange, remember there's another way to do it.

1.3. Step 3: Call the Function

Finally, we call the function to start the game.

```
guessing_game()
```

1.4. Complete Code

```
import random

def guessing_game():
    secret_number = random.randint(1, 100)
    attempts = 0
    guessed = False

    print("Welcome to the Guessing Game!")
    print("I'm thinking of a number between 1 and
```

```
100.")

    while not guessed:
        guess = int(input("Guess the number: "))
        attempts += 1

        if guess == secret_number:
            print(f"Congratulations! You guessed
the number in {attempts} attempts.")
            guessed = True
        elif guess < secret_number:
            print("The number is higher.")
        else:
            print("The number is lower.")

guessing_game()
```

Code Example 91

2. Project 2: Crazy Story Creator

Let's create a program that generates funny stories by asking the user for some words. This is similar to the game "Mad Libs".

2.1. Step 1: Define the Main Function

We'll define a function called `crazy_story_creator` that will contain all the program logic.

```
def crazy_story_creator():
    print("Welcome to the Crazy Story Creator!")

    name = input("Give me a name: ")
    place = input("Give me a place: ")
    object = input("Give me an object: ")
    action = input("Give me an action: ")

    story = f"One day, {name} went to {place} with
a {object}. Suddenly, they decided to {action}. It
was an incredible adventure!"

    print("\nHere's your crazy story:")
    print(story)
```

Take Note! Using an **f-string** makes things much easier. By writing a single string with an `f` in front and including variables inside curly braces { }, we can seamlessly combine text and variables. This is one of those concepts we want to introduce so you start getting familiar with it. It's not essential, but in the future, it will make your work much easier.

2.2. Step 2: Call the Function

Finally, we call the function to start the program.

```
crazy_story_creator()
```

2.3. Complete Code

```
def crazy_story_creator():
    print("Welcome to the Crazy Story Creator!")

    name = input("Give me a name: ")
    place = input("Give me a place: ")
    object = input("Give me an object: ")
    action = input("Give me an action: ")

    story = f"One day, {name} went to {place} with
a {object}. Suddenly, they decided to {action}. It
was an incredible adventure!"

    print("\nHere's your crazy story:")
    print(story)

crazy_story_creator()
```

Code Example 92

3. Project 3: Basic Calculator

Let's create a basic calculator that can perform addition, subtraction, multiplication, and division.

3.1. Step 1: Define Functions for Operations

First, we'll define functions for each of the operations.

```
def add(a, b):
    return a + b
```

```
def subtract(a, b):
    return a - b

def multiply(a, b):
    return a * b

def divide(a, b):
    if b != 0:
        return a / b
    else:
        return "Error: Division by zero"
```

3.2. Step 2: Define the Main Function

Next, we'll define a function called calculator that will ask the user to choose an operation and enter two numbers, then call the corresponding function.

```
def calculator():
    print("Welcome to the Basic Calculator!")

    operation = input("Choose an operation (add,
subtract, multiply, divide): ").lower()
    num1 = float(input("Enter the first number: "))
    num2 = float(input("Enter the second number:
"))

    if operation == "add":
        print(f"The result is: {add(num1, num2)}")
    elif operation == "subtract":
        print(f"The  result  is:  {subtract(num1,
num2)}")
    elif operation == "multiply":
        print(f"The  result  is:  {multiply(num1,
num2)}")
    elif operation == "divide":
        print(f"The  result  is:  {divide(num1,
num2)}")
    else:
        print("Invalid operation")
```

3.3. Step 3: Call the Function

Finally, we call the function to start the program.

```
calculator()
```

3.4. Complete Code

```
def add(a, b):
    return a + b

def subtract(a, b):
    return a - b

def multiply(a, b):
    return a * b

def divide(a, b):
    if b != 0:
        return a / b
    else:
        return "Error: Division by zero"

def calculator():
    print("Welcome to the Basic Calculator!")

    operation = input("Choose an operation (add,
subtract, multiply, divide): ").lower()
    num1 = float(input("Enter the first number: "))
    num2 = float(input("Enter the second number:
"))

    if operation == "add":
        print(f"The result is: {add(num1, num2)}")
    elif operation == "subtract":
        print(f"The result is: {subtract(num1,
num2)}")
    elif operation == "multiply":
        print(f"The result is: {multiply(num1,
num2)}")
    elif operation == "divide":
        print(f"The result is: {divide(num1,
num2)}")
    else:
        print("Invalid operation")

calculator()
```

Code Example 93

4. Project 4: Lucky Number Generator

Let's create a program that generates a lucky number based on the user's name.

4.1. Step 1: Import the **random** Library

First, we need to import the random library.

```
import random
```

4.2. Step 2: Define the Main Function

We'll define a function called lucky_number that will ask the user for their name and generate a lucky number based on it.

```
def lucky_number():
    print("Welcome to the Lucky Number Generator!")

    name = input("What's your name? ")
    lucky_number = random.randint(1, 100)

    print(f"Hello, {name}. Your lucky number is
{lucky_number}.")
```

4.3. Step 3: Call the Function

Finally, we call the function to start the program.

```
lucky_number ()
```

4.4. Complete Code

```
import random

def lucky_number():
    print("Welcome to the Lucky Number Generator!")

    name = input("What's your name? ")
    lucky_number = random.randint(1, 100)

    print(f"Hello, {name}.  Your  lucky  number  is
{lucky_number}.")
```

```
lucky_number()
```

Code Example 94

5. Project 5: Unit Converter

Let's create a program that converts kilometers to miles.

5.1. Step 1: Define the Main Function

We'll define a function called km_to_miles_converter that will ask the user for a distance in kilometers and convert it to miles.

```
def km_to_miles_converter():
    print("Welcome  to  the  Kilometers  to  Miles
Converter!")

    km  =  float(input("Enter  the  distance  in
kilometers: "))
    miles = km * 0.621371

    print(f"{km} kilometers is equal to {miles}
miles.")
```

5.2. Step 2: Call the Function

Finally, we call the function to start the program.

```
km_to_miles_converter()
```

5.3. Complete Code

```
def km_to_miles_converter():
    print("Welcome  to  the  Kilometers  to  Miles
Converter!")

    km  =  float(input("Enter  the  distance  in
kilometers: "))
    miles = km * 0.621371

    print(f"{km} kilometers is equal to {miles}
miles.")
```

```
km_to_miles_converter()
```
Code Example 95

In this chapter, we've created several fun projects to help you practice everything you've learned so far. Keep exploring and enjoy the art of programming!

CHAPTER 8: WORKING WITH CREATIVE GRAPHICS

In this chapter, we'll learn how to draw graphics using Python's **Turtle** library. Turtle is a super fun library that allows us to draw shapes and patterns on the screen using a "turtle" that we control with Python commands.

1. Introduction to Turtle

Turtle is a Python library used to introduce kids to graphical programming. It's easy to use and lets you create graphics and drawings effortlessly.

1.1. Installing Turtle

The Turtle library comes preinstalled with Python, so you don't need to install anything extra. You can start using it right away.

1.2. Importing the Library

To use Turtle, we first need to import it into our program:

```
import turtle
```

2. Initial Setup

Before we start drawing, we need to make some initial

configurations.

- Example:

```python
import turtle

# Create a drawing window
window = turtle.Screen()
window.title("My First Turtle Drawing")
window.bgcolor("white")

# Create a turtle
my_turtle = turtle.Turtle()
my_turtle.shape("turtle")
my_turtle.color("blue")

turtle.done()
```

Code Example 96

In this example, we create a drawing window and a turtle that we'll use to draw. The final `turtle.done()` statement tells Python that we're finished drawing, and the window should stay open.

> **Important Note:** Sometimes, after running a Turtle example and trying to run it again, you might encounter errors due to interference between the previous and current runs. If this happens, simply try running the program again. If it still doesn't work, you might need to restart Spyder or the IDE you're using. Another way to reset is from the **Console menu**, selecting **Restart Kernel**. This will reset everything so the program can run as if it's a new session.

Additional Troubleshooting Steps (e.g., in Spyder):
1. Restart the Kernel in Spyder:
   - Go to the Console menu.
   - Select Restart Kernel.
   - This will reset Python's environment and clear any interference from previous runs.
2. Run the Script from a Terminal:
   - Save your script as a `.py` file.
   - Open a terminal or command prompt.
   - Navigate to the file's location.

- Run the script with `python your_script_name.py`.

Following these steps will help avoid common errors and ensure your experience with Turtle is as smooth as possible.

3. Drawing Basic Shapes

Let's learn to draw some basic shapes using Turtle.

3.1. Drawing a Circle

We can use the `circle` method to draw a circle.

```
my_turtle.circle(50)    # Draws a circle with a
radius of 50 units
```

3.2. Drawing a Square

We can use a `for` loop to draw a square.

```
for _ in range(4):
    my_turtle.forward(100)    # Move  forward  100
units
    my_turtle.right(90)      # Turn 90 degrees to
the right
```

> **Take Note!** In this `for` loop, there's no variable like `for letter in word`. Since we don't need to use numbers like `0, 1, 2,` and `3`, we don't assign them a name. Instead, we use an underscore `_`.

4. Moving the Turtle

We can move the turtle using the methods `forward`, `backward`, `left`, and `right`.

- Example:

```
my_turtle.forward(100)    # Move forward 100 units
my_turtle.right(90)       # Turn 90 degrees to the
right
my_turtle.forward(100)    # Move forward 100 units
my_turtle.right(90)       # Turn 90 degrees to the
right
```

```
my_turtle.forward(100)    # Move forward 100 units
my_turtle.right(90)       # Turn 90 degrees to the
right
my_turtle.forward(100)    # Move forward 100 units
```

5. Changing the Color

We can change the turtle's color and the fill color of the shapes it draws.

- Example:

```
my_turtle.color("red")        # Change the turtle's
color to red
my_turtle.begin_fill()        # Start filling the
shape
my_turtle.circle(50)          # Draw a circle with
a radius of 50 units
my_turtle.end_fill()          # Finish filling
the shape
```

6. Useful Commands

There are many useful commands for drawing with our turtle:

- my_turtle.forward(100): Moves the turtle forward 100 units.
- my_turtle.backward(100): Moves the turtle backward 100 units.
- my_turtle.right(90): Turns the turtle 90 degrees to the right.
- my_turtle.left(90): Turns the turtle 90 degrees to the left.
- my_turtle.penup(): Lifts the pen so the turtle moves without drawing.
- my_turtle.pendown(): Lowers the pen so the turtle starts drawing.
- my_turtle.goto(x, y): Moves the turtle to a specific position on the drawing window at coordinates (x, y).
- my_turtle.setheading(90): Sets the turtle's direction to a specific angle (e.g., 90 degrees).

- `my_turtle.circle(50)`: Draws a circle with a radius of 50 units.
- `my_turtle.begin_fill()`: Starts filling the shape being drawn.
- `my_turtle.end_fill()`: Stops filling the shape being drawn.
- `my_turtle.color("red")`: Changes the pen and fill color of the turtle to red.
- `my_turtle.shape("turtle")`: Changes the turtle's shape to "turtle" (other options include "arrow", "circle", "square", "triangle", "classic").
- `my_turtle.speed(1)`: Adjusts the turtle's movement speed (can be a number from 1 to 10, or "fastest", "fast", "normal", "slow", "slowest").
- `my_turtle.stamp()`: Leaves a copy of the turtle at its current position.
- `my_turtle.clear()`: Clears the drawings made by the turtle without moving it.
- `my_turtle.reset()`: Clears the drawings and resets the turtle to its initial position and state.
- `my_turtle.hideturtle()`: Makes the turtle invisible.
- `my_turtle.showturtle()`: Makes the turtle visible again.
- `turtle.bgcolor("white")`: Changes the background color of the drawing window to white.
- `turtle.title("My Turtle Drawing")`: Changes the title of the drawing window.
- `turtle.done()`: Indicates that drawing is complete and keeps the window open.

7. Drawing a House

Let's create a fun project where we'll draw a house using Turtle. This will help us practice what we've learned so far. We'll break it down into steps to draw each part of the house.

7.1. Step 1: Draw the Base of the House

First, we'll draw a square as the base of the house.

```
import turtle

window = turtle.Screen()
window.title("House Drawing")
window.bgcolor("white")

my_turtle = turtle.Turtle()
my_turtle.shape("turtle")
my_turtle.color("blue")

# Draw the base of the house
my_turtle.penup()
my_turtle.goto(-50, -50)  # Move the turtle to the
starting point of the base
my_turtle.pendown()
for _ in range(4):
    my_turtle.forward(100)
    my_turtle.left(90)
```

7.2. Step 2: Draw the Roof

Next, we'll draw a triangle for the roof of the house.

```
# Draw the roof of the house
my_turtle.goto(-50, 50)
my_turtle.goto(0, 100)
my_turtle.goto(50, 50)
```

7.3. Step 3: Draw the Door

Finally, we'll draw a small rectangle for the door of the house.

```
# Draw the door
my_turtle.penup()
my_turtle.goto(-15, -50)
my_turtle.pendown()
my_turtle.setheading(90)   # Ensure the turtle is
pointing upward
for _ in range(2):
    my_turtle.forward(40)
    my_turtle.right(90)
```

```
    my_turtle.forward(30)
    my_turtle.right(90)

turtle.done()
```

7.4. Complete Code

```
import turtle

window = turtle.Screen()
window.title("House Drawing")
window.bgcolor("white")

my_turtle = turtle.Turtle()
my_turtle.shape("turtle")
my_turtle.color("blue")

# Draw the base of the house
my_turtle.penup()
my_turtle.goto(-50, -50)
my_turtle.pendown()
for _ in range(4):
    my_turtle.forward(100)
    my_turtle.left(90)

# Draw the roof of the house
my_turtle.goto(-50, 50)
my_turtle.goto(0, 100)
my_turtle.goto(50, 50)

# Draw the door
my_turtle.penup()
my_turtle.goto(-15, -50)
my_turtle.pendown()
my_turtle.setheading(90)
for _ in range(2):
    my_turtle.forward(40)
    my_turtle.right(90)
    my_turtle.forward(30)
    my_turtle.right(90)

turtle.done()
```

Code Example 97

The result should look similar to what we created. Enjoy

drawing your house!

8. Project: Draw a Smiley Face

Let's draw a smiley face using Turtle.

8.1. Step 1: Draw the Face

First, we'll draw a large circle for the face.

```
import turtle

window = turtle.Screen()
window.title("Smiley Face")
window.bgcolor("white")

my_turtle = turtle.Turtle()
my_turtle.shape("turtle")
my_turtle.color("yellow")

# Draw the face
my_turtle.begin_fill()
my_turtle.circle(100)
my_turtle.end_fill()
```

8.2. Step 2: Draw the Eyes

Next, we'll draw two smaller circles for the eyes.

```
# Draw the first eye
my_turtle.penup()
my_turtle.goto(-40, 120)
```

```
my_turtle.pendown()
my_turtle.color("black")
my_turtle.begin_fill()
my_turtle.circle(10)
my_turtle.end_fill()

# Draw the second eye
my_turtle.penup()
my_turtle.goto(40, 120)
my_turtle.pendown()
my_turtle.color("black")
my_turtle.begin_fill()
my_turtle.circle(10)
my_turtle.end_fill()
```

8.3. Step 3: Draw the Mouth

Finally, we'll draw a semicircle for the mouth.

```
# Draw the mouth
my_turtle.penup()
my_turtle.goto(-40, 80)
my_turtle.pendown()
my_turtle.right(90)
my_turtle.circle(40, 180)  # Draw a semicircle
```

These are the pieces that make up our program. It's important to learn how to break down a program idea into smaller, simpler steps.

8.4. Complete Code

```
import turtle

window = turtle.Screen()
window.title("Smiley Face")
window.bgcolor("white")

my_turtle = turtle.Turtle()
my_turtle.shape("turtle")
my_turtle.color("yellow")

# Draw the face
my_turtle.begin_fill()
my_turtle.circle(100)
```

```
my_turtle.end_fill()

# Draw the first eye
my_turtle.penup()
my_turtle.goto(-40, 120)
my_turtle.pendown()
my_turtle.color("black")
my_turtle.begin_fill()
my_turtle.circle(10)
my_turtle.end_fill()

# Draw the second eye
my_turtle.penup()
my_turtle.goto(40, 120)
my_turtle.pendown()
my_turtle.color("black")
my_turtle.begin_fill()
my_turtle.circle(10)
my_turtle.end_fill()

# Draw the mouth
my_turtle.penup()
my_turtle.goto(-40, 80)
my_turtle.pendown()
my_turtle.right(90)
my_turtle.circle(40, 180)

turtle.done()
```

Code Example 98

Take a look at our result. Does it look like yours? ♻

9. Additional Exercises

To reinforce what you've learned, here are some extra exercises. Try solving them without looking at the solutions first.

9.1. Exercise 1: Draw a Triangle

1. Use a for loop to draw an equilateral triangle.
2. Each side of the triangle should be 100 units long.
    *   Solution:

```python
import turtle

window = turtle.Screen()
window.title("Draw a Triangle")
window.bgcolor("white")

my_turtle = turtle.Turtle()
my_turtle.shape("turtle")
my_turtle.color("green")

# Draw a triangle
for _ in range(3):
    my_turtle.forward(100)
    my_turtle.left(120)

turtle.done()
```

Code Example 99

9.2. Exercise 2: Draw a Star

1. Use a for loop to draw a 5-pointed star.
2. Each line of the star should be 100 units long.
    *   Solution:

```python
import turtle

window = turtle.Screen()
window.title("Draw a Star")
window.bgcolor("white")

my_turtle = turtle.Turtle()
my_turtle.shape("turtle")
my_turtle.color("purple")
```

```
# Draw a star
for _ in range(5):
    my_turtle.forward(100)
    my_turtle.right(144)

turtle.done()
```

Code Example 100

Your star should look something like this.

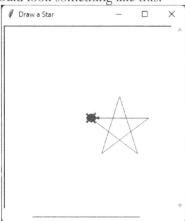

9.3. Exercise 3: Draw a Hexagon

1. Use a `for` loop to draw a hexagon.
2. Each side of the hexagon should be 80 units long.
    *   Solution:

```
import turtle

window = turtle.Screen()
window.title("Draw a Hexagon")
window.bgcolor("white")

my_turtle = turtle.Turtle()
my_turtle.shape("turtle")
my_turtle.color("blue")

# Draw a hexagon
for _ in range(6):
    my_turtle.forward(80)
```

```
    my_turtle.left(60)

turtle.done()
```

Code Example 101

In this chapter, we've learned how to use the Turtle library to draw graphics in Python. We've created several fun projects, like a house and a smiley face, and practiced drawing basic shapes. Keep going, stay creative, and enjoy the process of programming!

CHAPTER 9: EXPLORING MODULES

1. What is a Module?

A module in Python is a file that contains Python code, such as functions and variables, that you can reuse in other programs. Using modules allows you to take advantage of work done by other programmers and easily add new features to your programs.

2. Importing Modules

To use a module in your program, you need to import it. This is done using the `import` keyword.

- Example:

```
import math
```

In this example, we're importing the `math` module, which contains many useful mathematical functions.

3. Using Functions from a Module

Once you've imported a module, you can use the functions and variables defined in it.

- Example:

```
import math
```

```
number = 16
square_root = math.sqrt(number)
print("The square root of", number, "is",
square_root)
```
Code Example 102

In this example, we use the `sqrt` function from the `math` module to calculate the square root of a number.

4. Exploring the `math` Module

The `math` module is very helpful for performing advanced mathematical operations. Here are some of the most common functions:

- `math.sqrt(x)`: Returns the square root of x.
- `math.pow(x, y)`: Returns x raised to the power of y.
- `math.pi`: Returns the value of pi (π) approximately.
- `math.sin(x)`, `math.cos(x)`, `math.tan(x)`: Returns the sine, cosine, and tangent of x (where x is in radians). If you don't know what all of these things are yet, don't worry! This is just to show you that this library has a ton of useful math functions.
- Example:

```
import math

print("The value of pi is:", math.pi)
print("2 raised to the power of 3 is:", math.pow(2,
3))
print("The sine of 90 degrees is:",
math.sin(math.radians(90)))
```
Code Example 103

5. The `random` Module

The `random` module is very useful for working with random numbers. You can use it to make games, simulations, and much more.

- Example:

```
import random

random_number = random.randint(1, 100)
print("Random number between 1 and 100:",
random_number)
```
Code Example 104

In this example, we use the `randint` function from the `random` module to generate a random number between 1 and 100.

6. Exploring the `random` Module

The `random` module has many useful functions:

- `random.randint(a, b)`: Returns a random integer between a and b.
- `random.choice(seq)`: Returns a random element from the sequence `seq`.
- `random.shuffle(seq)`: Randomly shuffles the elements in the sequence `seq`.
- `random.random()`: Returns a random floating-point number between 0.0 and 1.0.
- Example:

```
import random

# List of fruits
fruits = ["apple", "banana", "cherry", "orange"]

# Choose a random fruit
random_fruit = random.choice(fruits)
print("Random fruit:", random_fruit)

# Shuffle the list of fruits
random.shuffle(fruits)
print("Shuffled fruits:", fruits)
```
Code Example 105

7. Creating Your Own Modules

You can also create your own modules. This is useful when you have functions you want to reuse across multiple programs.

7.1. Step 1: Create a Module

Create a file called `my_functions.py` and define some functions in it. Make sure to save this file in the same folder as your main program.

```
# File: my_functions.py

def greet(name):
    print("Hello, " + name + "!")

def say_goodbye(name):
    print("Goodbye, " + name + "!")
```
Code example File: `my_functions.py`

7.2. Step 2: Import and Use the Module

Create another file called `main_program.py` in the same folder and use the functions from the module you created.

```
# File: main_program.py

import my_functions

my_functions.greet("Anna")
my_functions.say_goodbye("Anna")
```
Code Example 106

When you run `main_program.py`, you'll see the following output:

```
Hello, Anna!
Goodbye, Anna!
```

Note: It's important that both files are in the same folder so Python can find and use the module.

8. Exploring Useful Modules for Kids

There are many Python modules that are especially useful and fun for kids. Some require installation, but many come preinstalled. Here are a few:

8.1. `time` Module

The `time` module is useful for working with time. You can use it to pause your program for a while or measure how long something takes to run.

- Example:

```
import time

print("Wait for 3 seconds...")
time.sleep(3)
print("Done!")
```

Code Example 107

8.2. `datetime` Module

The datetime module lets you work with dates and times.

- Example:

```
import datetime

current_date = datetime.datetime.now()
print("Current date and time:", current_date)
```

Code Example 108

8.3. `os` Module

The os module allows you to interact with the operating system. You can use it to create, delete, and list files and directories. This is a bit advanced but very useful for the future.

- Example:

```
import os

current_directory = os.getcwd()
print("Current directory:", current_directory)

# List files in the current directory
files = os.listdir(current_directory)
print("Files in the current directory:", files)
```

Code Example 109

9. List of Useful Modules

- **random**: Allows you to generate random numbers and choose random elements, perfect for creating games and simulations.

- **math**: Provides advanced mathematical functions like square root calculations, powers, and trigonometry.
- **pygame**: A library for creating video games, offering tools to handle graphics, sounds, and keyboard or mouse events.
- **numpy**: Used for working with arrays and performing complex mathematical calculations, very useful in data science and simulations.
- **turtle**: Lets you draw graphics and shapes on the screen in a fun and easy way, ideal for learning basic programming concepts.
- **time**: Offers functions to measure time and pause program execution, great for creating time effects in games.
- **os**: Provides functions to interact with the operating system, such as managing files and directories.
- **sys**: Allows you to interact with the system and Python's runtime environment, useful for handling command-line arguments and controlling program output.
- **datetime**: Makes it easier to work with dates and times, enabling you to create calendars, timers, and schedule tasks.
- **matplotlib**: Used to create graphs and data visualizations, ideal for learning how to represent information visually.
- **tkinter**: A library for creating graphical user interfaces (GUIs), allowing you to design windows, buttons, and other interactive elements.
- **json**: Simplifies working with data in JSON (JavaScript Object Notation) format, useful for saving and sharing structured information.
- **re**: Provides tools to work with regular expressions, useful for searching and manipulating text in advanced ways.
- **collections**: Offers additional data types like ordered

lists and dictionaries with multiple values, extending the capabilities of Python's standard data structures.

- **itertools**: Provides functions for creating efficient iterators, useful for performing combinations, permutations, and other advanced iteration operations.

10. More Examples and Exercises with Modules

Let's explore more examples and exercises to practice using modules in Python.

10.1. Example 1: Using the `math` Module to Calculate the Area of a Circle

We'll write a program to calculate the area of a circle using the `math` module.

```python
import math

def calculate_circle_area(radius):
    return math.pi * (radius ** 2)

radius = float(input("Enter the radius of the
circle: "))
area = calculate_circle_area(radius)
print(f"The area of the circle with radius
{radius} is {area}")
```

Code Example 110

10.2. Example 2: Using the `random` Module to Create a List of Random Numbers

We'll write a program that generates a list of 5 random numbers between 1 and 100.

```python
import random

random_numbers = [random.randint(1, 100) for _ in
range(5)]
print("List of random numbers:", random_numbers)
```

Code Example 111

11. Additional Exercises

To strengthen your understanding, here are some additional exercises. Try solving them without looking at the solutions first!

11.1. Exercise 1: Create a Greeting Module

1. Create a file called greetings.py and define a function called personalized_greeting that takes a name as a parameter and greets the person.
2. Import the function into a main program and use it to greet two different people.
   - Solution:

```
# File: greetings.py

def personalized_greeting(name):
    print("Hello, " + name + "! Welcome.")
```

Code example File: greetings.py

```
# File: main_program.py

import greetings

greetings.personalized_greeting("John")
greetings.personalized_greeting("Maria")
```

Code Example 112

11.2. Exercise 2: Create a Math Module

1. Create a module called math_operations.py that contains a function average that takes a list of numbers and returns their average.
2. Import the function into a main program and use it to calculate the average of a list of numbers.
   - Solution:

```
# File: math_operations.py

def average(numbers):
    return sum(numbers) / len(numbers)
```

Code example File: math_operations.py

```
# File: main_program.py

import math_operations

numbers = [10, 20, 30, 40, 50]
result = math_operations.average(numbers)
print("The average is:", result)
```
Code Example 113

11.3. Exercise 3: Create a Module for Random Numbers

1. Create a module called `random_numbers.py` that contains a function `generate_list` that takes two parameters, `n` and `max_value`, and returns a list of `n` random numbers between 1 and `max_value`.
2. Import the function into a main program and use it to generate a list of 10 random numbers between 1 and 100.
   - Solution:

```
# File: random_numbers.py

import random

def generate_list(n, max_value):
    return [random.randint(1, max_value) for _ in
range(n)]
```
Code example File: random_numbers.py

```
# File: main_program.py

import random_numbers

random_list  =  random_numbers.generate_list(10,
100)
print("List of random numbers:", random_list)
```
Code Example 114

11.4. Exercise 4: Create a Unit Conversion Module

1. Create a module called `unit_conversion.py` that contains a function `km_to_miles` to convert kilometers to miles (1 km = 0.621371 miles).

87

2. Import the function into a main program and use it to convert a distance in kilometers to miles.

- Solution:

```
# File: unit_conversion.py

def km_to_miles(km):
    return km * 0.621371
```

Code example File: `unit_conversion.py`

```
# File: main_program.py

import unit_conversion

kilometers = float(input("Enter the distance in kilometers: "))
miles = unit_conversion.km_to_miles(kilometers)
print(f"{kilometers} kilometers is equal to {miles} miles")
```

Code Example 115

11.5. Wrapping Up

In this chapter, we've learned about modules in Python: what they are, how to import and use them, and how to create our own modules. We also explored some useful modules that you can use in your programs and practiced with various exercises. Keep progressing and enjoy every moment of your programming adventure!

CHAPTER 10: CREATING A FINAL PROJECT

In this chapter, we're going to create a final project that combines everything we've learned so far. This project will be a simple game that you can customize and improve. First, we'll talk about how to plan your project, then how to implement it, and finally how to review and improve it.

1. Project Planning

Before you start programming, it's important to plan your project. Planning helps you understand what you want to achieve and how you're going to do it. Here are some steps to plan your programming project.

1.1. Step 1: Define the Goal of Your Project

First, decide what kind of project you want to make. It could be a game, a simple app, or anything else that interests you. In this chapter, we'll create a simple game called *"Guess the Number"*.

1.2. Step 2: Break the Project into Smaller Tasks

Break your project into smaller, manageable tasks. This will help you stay organized and not feel overwhelmed. Here are the main tasks for our game:

1. Generate a random number.
2. Ask the user to guess the number.
3. Give hints to the user (e.g., "The number is higher" or "The number is lower").
4. Count the number of attempts the user makes.
5. Congratulate the user when they guess the number correctly.

1.3. Step 3: Plan the User Interface

Decide how you'll interact with the user. In this case, we'll use the `input` function to ask the user for their guesses and the `print` function to give them hints and helpful messages. The game should be fun —if we don't help the user, it could become boring.

1.4. Step 4: Draw a Flowchart

A flowchart is a drawing that shows the steps your program will follow. Here's a simple flowchart for our game:

```
[Start] -> [Generate a random number] -> [Ask user
for a guess] -> [Is the guess correct?]
  -> [Yes] -> [Congratulate the user] -> [End]
  -> [No] -> [Is the number higher or lower?] ->
[Give a hint] -> [Repeat]
```

This plan will help guide you as you write your program.

2. Implementing the Project

Now that we've planned our project, it's time to start programming. Let's walk you through creating our *"Guess the Number"* game step by step.

2.1. Step 1: Import Necessary Modules

We'll use the `random` module to generate a random number.

```
import random
```

2.2. Step 2: Generate a Random Number

We'll generate a random number between 1 and 100.

```
secret_number = random.randint(1, 100)
```

2.3. Step 3: Ask the User to Guess the Number

We'll use a `while` loop to ask the user to guess the number until they guess correctly.

```
attempts = 0
guessed = False

print("Welcome to the Guess the Number game!")
print("I'm thinking of a number between 1 and
100.")

while not guessed:
    guess = int(input("Guess the number: "))
    attempts += 1

    if guess == secret_number:
        print(f"Congratulations! You guessed the
number in {attempts} attempts.")
        guessed = True
    elif guess < secret_number:
        print("The number is higher.")
    else:
        print("The number is lower.")
```

2.4. Complete Code

Here's the complete code for our *"Guess the Number"* game.

```
import random

def guessing_game():
    secret_number = random.randint(1, 100)
    attempts = 0
    guessed = False

    print("Welcome to the Guess the Number game!")
    print("I'm thinking of a number between 1 and
100.")

    while not guessed:
```

```
        guess = int(input("Guess the number: "))
        attempts += 1

        if guess == secret_number:
            print(f"Congratulations! You guessed
the number in {attempts} attempts.")
            guessed = True
        elif guess < secret_number:
            print("The number is higher.")
        else:
            print("The number is lower.")

guessing_game()
```

Code Example 116

3. Review and Improvements

Once you've created your project, it's important to review it and think about how you could improve it. Here are some ideas to enhance our *"Guess the Number"* game.

3.1. Idea 1: Set an Attempt Limit

We can set a limit on the number of attempts to make the game more challenging. If the user doesn't guess the number within a certain number of attempts, they lose the game.

- Example:

```
import random

def guessing_game():
    secret_number = random.randint(1, 100)
    attempts = 0
    attempt_limit = 10
    guessed = False

    print("Welcome to the Guess the Number game!")
    print("I'm thinking of a number between 1 and
100.")
    print(f"You have {attempt_limit} attempts to
guess the number.")

    while not guessed and attempts < attempt_limit:
        guess = int(input("Guess the number: "))
        attempts += 1
```

```
        if guess == secret_number:
            print(f"Congratulations! You guessed
the number in {attempts} attempts.")
            guessed = True
        elif guess < secret_number:
            print("The number is higher.")
        else:
            print("The number is lower.")

    if not guessed:
        print(f"Sorry, you've reached the attempt
limit. The secret number was {secret_number}.")

guessing_game()
```

Code Example 117

Did you know? if not guessed: means "if you haven't guessed the number," which is the same as if guessed == False. Therefore, guessed == False can always be rewritten as not guessed, since guessed is either True or False.

3.2. Idea 2: Allow the User to Choose the Number Range

We can let the user choose the range of numbers they want to play with.

- Example:

```
import random

def guessing_game():
    print("Welcome to the Guess the Number game!")
    min_number = int(input("Enter the minimum
number of the range: "))
    max_number = int(input("Enter the maximum
number of the range: "))
    secret_number = random.randint(min_number,
max_number)
    attempts = 0
    attempt_limit = 10
    guessed = False

    print(f"I'm thinking of a number between
{min_number} and {max_number}.")
```

```
    print(f"You have {attempt_limit} attempts to
guess the number.")

    while not guessed and attempts < attempt_limit:
        guess = int(input("Guess the number: "))
        attempts += 1

        if guess == secret_number:
            print(f"Congratulations! You guessed
the number in {attempts} attempts.")
            guessed = True
        elif guess < secret_number:
            print("The number is higher.")
        else:
            print("The number is lower.")

    if not guessed:
        print(f"Sorry, you've reached the attempt
limit. The secret number was {secret_number}.")

guessing_game()
```

Code Example 118

4. Final Exercise

Now it's your turn to improve the game! Here are some ideas for you to practice:
1. **Add Difficulty Levels**: Let the user choose between different difficulty levels (easy, medium, hard), where each level has a different number range and attempt limit.
2. **Save High Scores**: Save the highest score (the fewest attempts needed to guess the number) and display it at the end of the game.
3. **Add Motivational Messages**: Include motivational messages or extra hints to make the game more interactive.

4.1. Solution to the Final Exercise

Here's one possible solution that incorporates the suggested improvements:

```
import random

def guessing_game():
```

```
    print("Welcome to the Guess the Number game!")
    print("Choose a difficulty level:")
    print("1. Easy (numbers between 1 and 10, 5
attempts)")
    print("2. Medium (numbers between 1 and 50, 7
attempts)")
    print("3. Hard (numbers between 1 and 100, 10
attempts)")

    level = int(input("Enter the number of your
choice (1, 2, or 3): "))

    if level == 1:
        min_number, max_number, attempt_limit = 1,
10, 5
    elif level == 2:
        min_number, max_number, attempt_limit = 1,
50, 7
    else:
        min_number, max_number, attempt_limit = 1,
100, 10

    secret_number  =  random.randint(min_number,
max_number)
    attempts = 0
    guessed = False

    print(f"I'm thinking of a number between
{min_number} and {max_number}.")
    print(f"You have {attempt_limit} attempts to
guess the number.")

    while not guessed and attempts < attempt_limit:
        guess = int(input("Guess the number: "))
        attempts += 1

        if guess == secret_number:
            print(f"Congratulations! You guessed
the number in {attempts} attempts.")
            guessed = True
        elif guess < secret_number:
            print("The number is higher.")
        else:
            print("The number is lower.")

    if not guessed:
        print(f"Sorry, you've reached the attempt
```

```
limit. The secret number was {secret_number}.")

guessing_game()
```
Code Example 119

5. Chapter Summary

In this chapter, we learned how to plan a programming project, how to implement it, and how to review and improve it. We created a simple game called "Guess the Number" and explored ways to enhance it. Keep programming and enjoy every challenge!

FINAL CHAPTER: THE BEGINNING OF YOUR PROGRAMMING ADVENTURE!

Congratulations! You've reached the end of this book and learned so much about programming in Python. Now, with the skills and knowledge you've gained, you can create many exciting things. This is just the beginning of your journey into the world of programming.

1. Do You Realize What You Can Do?

With everything you've learned, you now have a solid foundation to create your own projects. Here are some ideas for what you can do:

1.1. Create Simple Games

You already know how to use conditionals, loops, functions, and user input. With these skills, you can create simple games like:

- **Guess the Number**: Improve the game we made in the final project by adding more levels, scores, and other features.
- **Quiz Game**: Create a game that asks questions and checks the player's answers.
- **Rock, Paper, Scissors**: Program a game where you play against the computer.

1.2. Create Useful Applications

You can also create useful apps to help you in your daily life:

- **Calculator**: A calculator that can add, subtract, multiply, and divide.
- **Unit Converter**: An app that converts units like kilometers to miles, Celsius to Fahrenheit, and more.
- **Contact Book**: A program where you can save and search for information about your friends and family.

2. Do You Think Everything You've Learned Doesn't Have Practical Applications in Real Life?

What you've learned is just the beginning. With some additional knowledge, you can do even more amazing things.

2.1. Program Games with Graphics

Using the `turtle` library you learned about in Chapter 8, you can create graphics and drawings. With other libraries like **pygame**, you can make games with more advanced graphics.

- Example:
- **Snake Game**: A classic game where you control a snake that grows as it eats food, while avoiding crashing into walls or itself.

2.2. Create Web Applications

By learning a little HTML, CSS, and JavaScript, along with Python frameworks like Flask or Django, you can create your own web pages and web applications.

- Example:
- **Personal Blog**: You can create a website to share your thoughts, stories, and photos.

2.3. Work with Data and Data Science

With libraries like **pandas**, **numpy**, and **matplotlib**, you can learn to work with data, create graphs, and perform data analysis.

- Example:

- **Survey Data Analysis**: You can take survey data and analyze it to see people's opinions on different topics.

3. Continuing Your Learning

Here are some resources to keep learning and exploring:
- **Books and Online Tutorials**: There are many books and online tutorials available to teach you more about Python and other programming languages.
- **Online Courses**: Platforms like Coursera, edX, and Khan Academy offer free courses on programming.
- **Programming Communities**: Join online communities like Stack Overflow, GitHub, and programming forums where you can ask questions and learn from other programmers.

4. A Second Book in This Collection Is Coming Soon!

Don't forget, a second book in this collection will be available soon, so keep practicing to follow along with ease! This next book will take you even further on your programming journey, exploring more advanced topics and exciting projects.

5. Final Motivation

Programming is a powerful skill that allows you to create amazing things and solve problems. With every project you make, you learn something new and improve your abilities. Here are some reasons to keep programming:
- **Creativity**: Programming lets you express your creativity in unique ways. You can create games, apps, and websites that reflect your interests and personality.
- **Problem-Solving**: Programming teaches you to think logically and solve problems efficiently.
- **Career Opportunities**: Programming is a highly in-demand skill in the job market. Many careers in technology, science, engineering, and business require programming knowledge.
- **Fun**: Programming is fun! It's exciting to see your

ideas come to life on your computer screen.

6. Keep Exploring and Creating!

Remember, the key to improving is to keep practicing and exploring. Don't be afraid to make mistakes; every mistake is an opportunity to learn something new. Keep going, have fun programming, and never stop exploring!

---

7. A Farewell Message

Dear reader,

We hope you've enjoyed this journey into the world of programming as much as we enjoyed creating it for you. Now, you have the tools and knowledge to start creating your own projects and exploring new ideas. Programming is an exciting adventure that's just beginning. We're confident you'll create amazing things!

Good luck and happy programming!

Carlos Roldán Blay and Marta Roldán Canti

ABOUT THE AUTHORS

Carlos Roldán Blay is a Doctor of Industrial Engineering specializing in electrical engineering, with a deep passion for learning new things and sharing his knowledge. His interest in technology and education has led him to explore the world of programming and teach others in an accessible and fun way. In addition to his love for engineering and programming, Carlos has many hobbies —he is a pianist and a mathematician— but his greatest joy is dedicating time to his family as a devoted husband and father. This book is a special project created alongside his daughter, aiming to inspire young minds to discover the fascinating world of programming.

Marta Roldán Canti, at just 10 years old, is a curious and enthusiastic girl eager to learn and try everything. Her energy and creativity make her an exceptional co-author for this project. Marta reviewed and improved every chapter of the book, offering her unique perspective and ensuring it's accessible and fun for other kids. Her passion for technology and adventurous spirit are the driving forces behind this book, and she's excited to share this thrilling journey with other young programmers. In the future, who knows? This budding violinist and potential equestrian might become a great programmer. Only time will tell!

NOTES

We've left this space for you to write down what you're learning. All the code examples in the book are numbered, so you can note which example contains something you want to remember. Write it here! You can also jot down the chapter, page number, or even rewrite the entire example with your own notes or modifications. We hope this space is helpful for you!

Carlos Roldán Blay and Marta Roldán Canti

To be continued…